Restaurant Copycat Cookbook

Quick And Easy Delicious Dishes To Prepare At Home From Your Favorite Restaurant.

Sommario

Introduction

Sometimes you have no idea what to cook and prepare, always becoming boring to cook...So why not have some fun in the kitchen by preparing the dishes you love from your favorite restaurants? Just think of all the money you'll save by not driving, paying for your meals, and tipping your waiter! Dining out is expensive and can cost you $16 or more per meal than if you had eaten at home. Plus, when you cook at home, you have full control over what will be on your plate, and the taste will make you appreciate home cooked food. Nothing compares to homemade food. It's fresh, it's tasty, and you can eat as much as you want since you control the quantities.

If you're wondering where you can find these recipes or are worried because you're not really a "chef" in the kitchen, don't worry, I've got you covered. This book contains detailed recipes and instructions on how to cook the most popular recipes from some of the best restaurants.

Put on your apron and let's get started....

Chapter 1: Breakfast

IHOP's Banana Bread

Preparation Time: 15 minutes

Cooking Time: 30 minutes

Serving: 4

Ingredients:

Four slices of banana bread

One banana sliced

Four teaspoons butter

Four tablespoons caramel sauce

Two eggs

Two tablespoons milk

Two tablespoons whipped cream

Nutmeg optional

Directions:

Whisk one egg and one spoonful of milk together and dump the whisked egg into a shallow bowl. Heat a pan over medium heat and put in the pan around one teaspoon butter.

Place one slice of banana bread into the mixture of the eggs, coat evenly, turn over the bread and then do the coating on the other side of the loaf. Put the bread in the skillet and cook at each side for about 1 minute. Place the bread on a plate, slice the banana 1/2 and put on the toast.

Drizzle the French toast with caramel sauce, then top with some whipped cream.

IHOP's Healthy "Harvest Grain 'N Nut" Pancakes

Preparation Time: 5 Minutes

Cooking Time: 5 Minutes

Servings: 4

Ingredients:

1 teaspoon olive oil

¾ cup oats, powdered

¾ cup whole wheat flour

½ teaspoon salt

1½ cup buttermilk

¼ cup vegetable oil

1 egg

¼ cup sugar

3 tablespoons almonds, finely sliced

3 tablespoons walnuts, sliced

Syrup for serving

Directions:

Heat oil in a pan over medium heat.

As pan preheats, pulverize oats in a blender until powdered. Then, add to a large bowl with flour, baking soda, baking powder and salt. Mix well.

Add buttermilk, oil, egg, and sugar in a separate bowl. Mix with an electric mixer until creamy.

Mix in wet ingredients with dry ingredients, then add nuts. Mix everything together with electric mixer.

Scoop ⅓ cup of batter and cook in the hot pan for at least 2 minutes or until both sides turn golden brown. Transfer onto a plate, then repeat for the remaining batter.

Serve with syrup.

Copycat Power Breakfast Sandwich from Panera

Preparation Time: 10 minutes

Cooking Time: 7 minutes

Servings: 1

Ingredients:

2 egg whites

1 teaspoon butter, divided in half

1 bagel thin, cut in half

Mustard

¼ avocado, sliced

1 large tomato slice

4 spinach leaves

1 slice Swiss cheese

Directions:

Cook egg whites for about 1 minute in a small tightly covered custard cup in the microwave.

Apply ½ teaspoon butter onto both bagel thin halves. Coat inside of top bagel half with mustard and the other with avocado. Place egg whites, tomato, spinach leaves, and cheese on bottom bagel thin. Top with another bagel thin half.

Coat a heated pan with thin layer of cooking spray, pan fry sandwich on medium-high heat for 3 minutes on each side or until golden brown and cheese is melted. I use a panini press for this step.

Serve immediately.

Jimmy Dean's Homemade Pork Sage Sausage

Preparation Time: 10 minutes

Cooking time: 40 minutes

Servings: 8

Ingredients:

1 pound ground pork

1 teaspoon salt

½ teaspoon dried parsley

¼ teaspoon rubbed sage

¼ teaspoon black pepper, ground

¼ teaspoon dried thyme

¼ teaspoon coriander

¼ teaspoon seasoned salt

Directions:

Mix all ingredients in a bowl.

Shape into patties. Then, cook in a pan on medium heat until meat is brown on both sides and cooked through.

Serve.

DIY California A.M. Crunchwrap

Preparation Time: 10 minutes
Cooking Time: 20 minutes
Servings: 4

Ingredients:

4 frozen hash brown patties

5 large eggs

1 tablespoon milk

Salt and pepper, to taste

4 large tortillas

1 cup cheddar cheese, shredded

4 strips of thick cut bacon, cooked and crumbled

2 ripe California avocados, peeled and pitted

4 tablespoons pico de gallo

Directions:

Cook hash brown patties until crisp, based on package instructions.

Add eggs, milk, salt, and pepper in a bowl. Mix well until combined. Then, pour onto a skillet and cook until scrambled. Set aside.

Heat two different-sized (one smaller than other) heavy bottomed pans over medium heat. Once heated, place tortillas into the bigger pan and, in even amounts, add cheese, a hash brown patty, eggs, bacon, avocado, and pico de gallo in the center of the tortilla in that order.

Using a wheel pattern, fold tortilla around the filling with the edge facing up. Place heated smaller pan (such as a cast iron skillet) on top for about 20 seconds or until browned.

Serve immediately.

Buttermilk Pancake

Preparation Time: 5 minutes

Cooking Time: 8 minutes

Servings: 8 to 10

Ingredients:

1¼ cups all-purpose flour

1¼ cups granulated sugar

1 pinch salt

1 egg

1¼ cups buttermilk

¼ cup cooking oil

Directions:

Preheat your pan by leaving it over medium heat while you are preparing the pancake batter.

Take all of your dry ingredients and mix them together.

Take all of your wet ingredients and mix them together.

Carefully combine the dry mixture into the wet mixture until everything is mixed together completely.

Melt some butter in your pan.

Slowly pour batter into the pan until you have a 5-inch circle.

Flip the pancake when its edges seem to have hardened.

Cook the other side of the pancake until it is golden brown.

Repeat steps six through eight until your batter is finished.

Serve with softened butter and maple syrup.

Kiwi Muffins

Preparation Time: 10 Minutes

Cooking Time: 20 Minutes

Servings: 8-12

Ingredients:

1 cup milk

1 tablespoon olive oil

2 cups whole wheat flour

1 tsp baking soda

¼ tsp baking soda

1 tsp cinnamon 2 eggs

1 cup kiwi

Directions:

In a bowl combine all dry ingredients. In another bowl combine all dry ingredients

Combine wet and dry ingredients together

Pour mixture into 8-12 prepared muffin cups, fill 2/3 of the cups

Bake for 18-20 minutes at 375 F

When ready remove from the oven and serve

Chapter 2: Appetizers

Chili's Classic Nachos

Preparation Time: 25 minutes

Cooking Time: 2 hours & 10 minutes

Servings: 5

Ingredients:

2 tablespoons guacamole

1 boneless chicken breast, uncooked, cut in strips

A bag of tortilla chips, any of your choice

1 cup fresh lettuce, shredded

½ cup Monterey Jack cheese, shredded

1 package of fajita seasoning mix (1 ounce)

½ cup sharp cheddar cheese, shredded

1 jalapeño, sliced

½ cup your choice salsa

1 Vidalia onion, sliced

2 tablespoons low-fat sour cream

1 bell pepper, sliced

Directions:

Over moderate heat in a large skillet; sauté the chicken with onion, fajita seasoning & peppers. When done;

drain the prepared fajita mixture & set aside until ready to use.

Now, spread the tortillas out on your ovenproof platter in a large circle. Once done; start layering them with chicken, peppers and onions. Add the cheeses followed by the jalapenos. Place the platter into the oven & bake until the cheese is completely melted, for 5 to 10 minutes, at 350 F. Once done; pull out the platter & add the shredded lettuce in the center of chip circle. Top the lettuce with sour cream, salsa & guacamole. Serve immediately & enjoy.

Burger King Zesty Sauce

Preparation Time: 5 minutes

Cooking Time: 0 minutes

Servings: 10

Ingredients:

1/2 cup mayonnaise

2 teaspoons prepared horseradish

1 teaspoon cayenne pepper

1 teaspoon prepared mustard

1 teaspoon white vinegar

1 teaspoon lemon juice

1/4 teaspoon salt

1/4 teaspoon sugar

2 teaspoons ketchup

1 drop soy sauce

Directions:

Combine all ingredients in a bowl and stir until well blended.

Cover the bowl and refrigerate for 30 minutes before using.

Fried Pickles

Preparation Time: 5 minutes

Cooking Time: 10 minutes

Servings: 4

Ingredients:

2 cup pickle chips

¼ teaspoon cayenne pepper

1 teaspoon sugar

½ teaspoon pepper

2 cup flour

Oil, for frying

1 teaspoon salt

Directions:

Over moderate heat in a deep pan; heat the oil until hot. Now, in a large bowl; combine the flour together with cayenne, sugar, pepper, and salt; continue to whisk until combined well.

Drain the pickle chips & then toss them into the prepared flour mixture. Once done, work in batches and fry them (ensure that you don't overcrowd the pan). Once the pickles start to float to the surface, immediately remove them from the hot oil. Place them on paper towels to drain; serve with the horseradish or ranch dressing and enjoy.

Texas Chili Fries

Preparation Time: 10 minutes

Cooking Time: 20 minutes

Servings: 4

Ingredients:

1 package of bacon

1 bag cheese blend, shredded

Ranch salad dressing

1 bag steak fries, frozen

1 jar jalapeno peppers

Directions:

Evenly spread the fries over a large-sized cookie sheet & bake as per the directions mentioned on the package.

Line strips of bacon on a separate cookie sheet & bake until crispy.

When the bacon and fries are done; remove them from the oven.

Add a thick layer of jalapenos and cheese; crumble the bacon over the fries.

Bake in the oven again until the cheese is completely melted.

Serve hot with some Ranch salad dressing on side and enjoy.

Olive Garden Breadsticks

Preparation Time: 10 minutes

Cooking time: 45 minutes

Servings: 8

Ingredients:

¼ cup of softened butter

1 ½ teaspoons of salt

3 cups of bread flour

1 cup + 1 tablespoon of warm water

¾ teaspoon of active dry yeast

2 tablespoons of granulated sugar

Toppings:

½ teaspoon of garlic salt

2 tablespoons of melted butter

Directions:

1) Pour the warm water into a small bowl and add in the sugar and yeast, letting them dissolve. Then let the mixture sit for 5 minutes or until foam forms on top.

2) In a large bowl, mix the flour with salt, then add the softened butter into the flour using a paddle from an electric mixer. Pour the yeast mixture over the flour mixture, and using a dough hook, blend the ingredients and then knead the dough for around 10 minutes.

3) Put the dough in a covered container, then let it sit for about 1 to 1 ½ hours until the dough doubles in size.

4) After the dough has doubled in size, take 2-ounce portions and roll them between your hands to form sticks that are 7-inches long. Place the sticks on a tray covered by parchment paper, cover, and let them sit for 1 to 1 ½ hours until the dough doubles in size again.

5) Prepare the oven by preheating it to 400 degrees.

6) Bake the sticks for around 12 minutes, or until they turn golden brown. Once ready, brush each breadstick with melted butter and sprinkle garlic salt on them.

Tip: Set aside plenty of time for this recipe so that the dough can rise as much as required.

Pei Wei's Vietnamese Chicken Salad Spring Roll

Preparation Time: 10 minutes

Cooking Time: 1 minute

Servings: 4-6

Ingredients:

Salad

Rice Wrappers

Green leaf lettuce like Boston Bibb lettuce

Napa cabbage, shredded

Green onions, chopped

Mint, chopped

Carrots, cut into 1-inch matchsticks

Peanuts

Chicken, diced and cooked, about 6 chicken tenders drizzled with soy sauce, honey, garlic powder, and red pepper flakes Lime dressing

2 tablespoons lime juice, about 1 lime

1½ teaspoons water

1 tablespoon sugar

1 teaspoon salt

Dash of pepper

3 tablespoons oil

Add everything but the oil to a small container or bowl and shake or stir until the sugar and salt are dissolved. Next, add the oil and shake well.

Peanut dipping sauce

2 tablespoons soy sauce

1 tablespoon rice wine vinegar

2 tablespoons brown sugar

¼ cup peanut butter

1 teaspoon chipotle Tabasco

1 teaspoon honey

1 teaspoon sweet chili sauce

1 teaspoon lime vinaigrette

Add all the ingredients to a small bowl and mix to combine thoroughly.

Directions:

In a large bowl, mix together all of the salad ingredients except for the rice wrappers and lettuce.

Place the rice wrappers in warm water for about 1 minute to soften.

Transfer the wrappers to a plate and top each with 2 pieces of lettuce.

Top the lettuce with the salad mixture and drizzle with the lime dressing. Fold the wrapper by tucking in the ends and then rolling.

Serve with lime dressing and peanut dipping sauce.

Takeout Dry Garlic Ribs

Preparation Time: 15 minutes

Cooking Time: 2 hours and 15 minutes

Servings: 4-6

Ingredients:

6 pounds pork ribs, silver skin removed and cut into individual ribs

1½ cups broth - 1½ cups brown sugar - ¼ cup soy sauce

12 cloves garlic, minced - ¼ cup yellow mustard

1 large onion, finely chopped - ¼ teaspoon salt

½ teaspoon black pepper

Directions:

Preheat oven to 200°F.

Season ribs with salt and pepper and place on a baking tray. Cover with aluminum foil and bake for 1 hour.

In a mixing bowl, stir together the broth, brown sugar, soy sauce, garlic, mustard and onion. Continue stirring until the sugar is completely dissolved.

After an hour, remove the foil from the ribs and turn the heat up to 350°F.

Carefully pour the sauce over the ribs. Re-cover with the foil and return to the oven for 1 hour.

Remove the foil and bake for 15 more minutes on each side.

Boston Market Mac n' Cheese

Preparation Time: 10 minutes
Cooking Time: 20 minutes
Servings: 6

Ingredients:

1 8-ounce package spiral pasta

2 tablespoons butter

2 tablespoons all-purpose flour

1 ¾ cups whole milk

1 ¼ cups diced processed cheese like Velveeta™

¼ teaspoon dry mustard

½ teaspoon onion powder

1 teaspoon salt

Pepper, to taste

Directions:

Cook pasta according to package instructions. Drain, then set aside.

To prepare sauce make the roux with four and butter over medium-low heat in a large deep skillet. Add milk and whisk until well blended. Add cheese, mustard, salt, and pepper. Keep stirring until smooth.

Once pasta is cooked, transfer to a serving bowl. Pour cheese mixture on top. Toss to combine.

Serve warm.

Cheddar's Santa Fe Spinach Dip

Preparation Time: 5 minutes

Cooking Time: 20 minutes

Servings: 6

Ingredients:

2 packages chopped spinach, frozen (10 ounces each)

1 cup heavy whipping cream

2.4 ounces Monterey jack cheese; cut it into 3 equal 2" long blocks

1 package cream cheese (8 oz)

2.4 ounces pepper jack cheese; cut it into 3 equal 2" long blocks

½ cup Sour Cream

2.4 ounces White American Cheese; cut it into 3 equal 2" long blocks

½ to 1 teaspoon salsa seasoning

2 teaspoon Alfredo sauce

1 cup mozzarella cheese

Pepper & salt to taste

Directions:

Over low-heat in a large pan; heat the chopped spinach until all the moisture is cooked out, for a couple of minutes, stirring frequently.

In the meantime, over moderate heat in a large pot; add in the cream cheese & 1 cup of heavy whipping cream; cook until the cheese is completely melted; ensure that you don't really bring it to a boil. Feel free to decrease the heat, if it starts to boil.

Once done; work in batches and start adding the Pepper Jack, Monterey Jack & White American cheeses. Continue to stir the ingredients & don't let it come to a boil.

Lastly add in the Mozzarella cheese and continue to cook.

Add 2 teaspoons of the Alfredo sauce and then add in the cooked spinach.

Add ½ cup of the sour cream; continue to mix until combined well.

Add salsa seasoning, pepper & salt to taste; stir well

Serve immediately with some tortilla chips & enjoy!

Chapter 3: Salads and Side Dishes

Tomato, Cucumber and Onion Salad

This Cracker Barrel recipe will remind you of summertime anytime you prepare it.

Preparation Time: 5 minutes
Cooking Time: 0 minutes
Servings: 6

Ingredients:

1 pound grape tomatoes

3 cucumbers, sliced

½ cup white onion, sliced thinly

1 cup white vinegar

2 tablespoons Italian dressing

½ cup sugar

Directions:

Whisk together the vinegar, sugar, and Italian dressing in a small bowl.

Add the cucumbers, tomatoes, and onions. Toss to coat. Cover with plastic wrap and refrigerate until ready to serve or for at least 1 hour before serving.

Roasted Tomato Sauce

Preparation time: 2 hours

Cooking time: 75 minutes

Servings: 4

Ingredients:

1 1/2 kilos of tomatoes

3 tablespoon extra-virgin olive oil

6 peeled garlic cloves

1/2 cup sliced onion

2 teaspoons Italian seasoning

1 teaspoon kosher salt

1/4 teaspoon freshly ground black pepper

3 tablespoons chopped basil

Optional: 2 tablespoons tomato paste

Optional: 500 g of pasta

Optional: 1/8 teaspoon chopped red pepper flakes

Directions:

Gather the ingredients of the roasted tomato sauce and preheat the oven to 150 ºC.

Wash the tomatoes, remove the stem and cut them into pieces of approximately 2 centimeters.

Mix the tomatoes in a large bowl with olive oil, sliced onion, rolled garlic cloves, Italian seasoning, salt, and ground black pepper.

Place the tomatoes in a single layer on a baking sheet and bake for 60 minutes. Put roasted tomatoes and condiments in a food processor or blender.

Mix well and transfer to a large saucepan and add chopped basil, red peppers, and tomato paste, if you use them. Bring the roasted tomato sauce over low heat, and cook for 15 minutes or until reduced and thickened.

Cook the pasta in boiling water with salt; drains Mix the drained hot pasta with the sauce and serve with garlic bread if you wish.

If you are not going to use the sauce immediately, place it in a container or in glass jars with a lid and refrigerate and consume for up to 3 days, or store it in the freezer for up to 4 months.

House Salad and Dressing

Preparation Time: 10 minutes

Cooking Time: 0

Servings: 12

Ingredients:

Salad

1 head iceberg lettuce

¼ small red onion, sliced thin

6–12 black olives, pitted

6 pepperoncini

2 small roma tomatoes, sliced

Croutons

¼ cup shredded or grated romano or parmesan cheese

Dressing:

1 packet Italian dressing mix

¾ cup vegetable/canola oil

¼ cup olive oil

1 tablespoon mayonnaise

⅓ cup white vinegar

¼ cup water

½ teaspoon sugar

½ teaspoon dried Italian seasoning

½ teaspoon salt

¼ teaspoon pepper

¼ teaspoon garlic powder

Directions:

To make the dressing, combine all ingredients in a small bowl. Thoroughly whisk together. Refrigerate for 1 hour to marinate.

Add the salad ingredient to a salad bowl. When ready to serve, add some of the dressing to the salad and toss to coat. Add grated cheese as a garnish as desired.

Store remaining dressing in an airtight container. Keep refrigerated and it can be stored for up to 3 weeks.

Santa Fe Crispers Salad

Preparation Time: 10 minutes

Cooking Time: 30 minutes

Servings: 4

Ingredients:

1 ½ pounds boneless skinless chicken breasts

1 tablespoon fresh cilantro, chopped

¾ cup Lawry's Santa Fe Chili Marinated with Lime and Garlic, divided

1 package (10 ounces) torn romaine lettuce, approximately 8 cups

2 tablespoons milk 1 cup black beans, drained and rinsed

½ cup sour cream 1 cup drained canned whole kernel corn

¼ cup red onion, chopped

1 medium avocado, cut into chunks

½ cup Monterey Jack, shredded

1 medium tomato, cut into chunks

Directions:

Place chicken in a large glass dish or resealable marinade plastic bag

Add approximately ½ cup of the Santa Fe marinade, turn several times until nicely coated

Refrigerate for 30 minutes or longer

Removed the chicken from marinade; get rid of the leftover marinade

Grill the chicken until cooked through, for 6 to 7 minutes per side, over medium heat; brushing with 2 tablespoons of the leftover marinade Cut the chicken into thin slices.

Combine the sour cream together with milk, leftover marinade and cilantro with wire whisk in medium-sized bowl until smooth Arrange lettuce on large serving platter

Top with the chicken, avocado, corn, beans, cheese, tomato and onion.

Serve with tortilla chips and dressing. Enjoy.

Chapter 4: Pasta

Chow Mein from Panda Express

Preparation Time: 5 minutes

Cooking Time: 30 minutes

Servings: 6

Ingredients:

8 quarts water

12 ounces Yakisoba noodles

¼ cup soy sauce

3 garlic cloves, finely chopped

1 tablespoon brown sugar

2 teaspoons ginger, grated

¼ teaspoon white pepper, ground

2 tablespoons olive oil

1 onion, finely chopped

3 celery stalks, sliced on the bias

2 cups cabbage, chopped

Directions:

In a pot, bring water to a boil. Cook Yakisoba noodles for about 1 minute until noodles separate. Drain and set aside.

Combine soy sauce, garlic, brown sugar, ginger, and white pepper in a bowl.

In a pan, heat oil on medium-high heat. Sauté onion and celery for 3 minutes or until soft. Add cabbage and stir-fry for an additional minute. Mix in noodles and soy sauce mixture. Cook for 2 minutes, stirring continuously until noodles are well-coated.

Transfer into bowls. Serve.

Pesto Cavatappi from Noodles & Company

Preparation Time: 5 minutes

Cooking Time: 20 minutes

Servings: 8

Ingredients:

4 quarts water

1 tablespoon salt

1-pound macaroni pasta

1 teaspoon olive oil

1 large tomato, finely chopped

4 ounces mushrooms, finely chopped

¼ cup chicken broth

¼ cup dry white wine

¼ cup heavy cream

1 cup pesto

1 cup Parmesan cheese, grated

Directions:

Add water and salt to a pot. Bring to a boil. Put in pasta and cook for 10 minutes or until al dente. Drain and set aside.

In a pan, heat oil. Sauté tomatoes and mushrooms for 5 minutes. Pour in broth, wine, and cream. Bring to a boil. Reduce heat to medium and simmer for 2 minutes or until mixture is thick. Stir in pesto and cook for another 2 minutes. Toss in pasta. Mix until fully coated.

Transfer onto plates and sprinkle with Parmesan cheese.

Rattlesnake Pasta from Pizzeria Uno

Preparation Time: 5 minutes

Cooking Time: 20 minutes

Servings: 6

Ingredients:

Pasta:

4 quarts

1 pound penne pasta

1 dash of salt

Chicken:

2 tablespoons butter

2 cloves garlic, finely chopped

½ tablespoon Italian seasoning

1 pound chicken breast, boneless and skinless, cut into small squares

Sauce:

4 tablespoons butter

2 cloves garlic, finely chopped

¼ cup all-purpose flour

1 tablespoon salt

¾ teaspoon white pepper

2 cups milk

1 cup half-and-half

¾ cup Parmesan cheese, shredded

8 ounces Colby cheese, shredded

3 jalapeno peppers, chopped

Directions:

In a pot of boiling water, add salt, and cook pasta according to package instructions. Drain well and set aside.

To prepare the chicken, heat butter in a pan. Sauté garlic and Italian seasoning for 1 minute. Add chicken and cook 5-7 minutes or until cooked thoroughly, flipping half way through. Transfer onto a plate once. Set aside.

In the same pan, prepare the sauce. Add butter and heat until melted. Stir in garlic and cook for 30 seconds. Then, add flour, salt, and pepper. Cook for 2 more minutes, stirring continuously. Pour in milk and half-and-half. Keep stirring until sauce turns thick and smooth.

Toss in chicken, jalapeno peppers, and pasta. Stir until combined.

Serve.

Chapter 5: Chicken

Cracker Barrel Chicken Potpie

Preparation Time: 5 minutes
Cooking Time: 30 minutes
Servings: 6

Ingredients:

Two tablespoons canola oil

One medium onion, chopped

1/2 cup all-purpose flour

One teaspoon poultry seasoning

3/4 cup 2% milk

One can (14-1/2 ounces) chicken broth

3 cups cubed cooked chicken

2 cups of frozen mixed vegetables, thawed

One sheet refrigerated pie crust

Directions:

Preheat the oven to 450 ° C. Heat oil in a large saucepan over medium-high heat. Add onion; stir and cook until tender. Season with flour and poultry until blended; whisk slowly in broth and milk. Shift to 9-inch grained deep-soaked pie plate; place the crust over the filling. Trim and seal the edges. In the crust put some slits. Bake for 15-20 minutes or until golden brown.

Double Chicken Pie

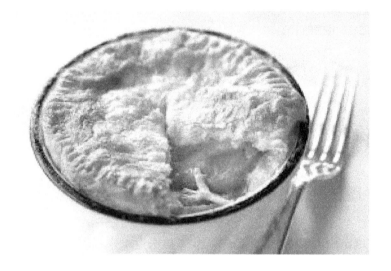

Preparation Time: 5 minutes

Cooking Time: 30 minutes

Servings: 6

Ingredients:

½ cup butter

1 medium onion, diced

1 (14.5-ounce) can chicken broth

1 cup half and half milk

½ cup all-purpose flour

1 carrot, diced

1 celery stalk, diced

3 medium potatoes, peeled and diced

3 cups cooked chicken, diced

½ cup frozen peas

1 teaspoon chicken seasoning

½ teaspoon salt

½ teaspoon ground pepper

1 single refrigerated pie crust

1 egg

Water

Directions:

Preheat the oven to 375°F.

In a large skillet, heat the butter over medium heat, add the leeks and sauté for 3 minutes.

Sprinkle flour over the mixture, and continue to stir constantly for 3 minutes.

Whisking constantly, blend in the chicken broth and milk. Bring the mixture to a boil. Reduce heat to medium-low.

Add the carrots, celery, potatoes, salt, pepper, and stir to combine. Cook for 10-15 minutes or until veggies are cooked through but still crisp. Add chicken and peas. Stir to combine.

Transfer chicken filling to a deep 9-inch pie dish.

Fit the pie crust sheet on top and press the edges around the dish to seal the crust. Trim the excess if needed.

In a separate bowl, whisk an egg with 1 tablespoon of water, and brush the mixture over the top of the pie. With a knife, cut a few slits to let steam escape.

Bake the pie in the oven on the middle oven rack 20 to 30 minutes until the crust becomes golden brown.

Let the pie rest for about 15 minutes before serving.

Chapter 6: Beef and Pork

Stuffed Pork Chop

Preparation Time: 15 minutes
Cooking Time: 3 hours 30 minutes
Serving: 4

Ingredients:

8 pork chops

½ pound sausages

2 cups rice, cooked

1 tablespoon chopped celery leaves

1 tablespoon sausage drippings

1 tablespoon chopped parsley

1 small onion, grated

1 teaspoon poultry seasoning

½ teaspoon salt

⅛ teaspoon pepper

Directions:

Preheat the oven to 350°F.

Slice each pork chop on one side to create a pocket.

Combine the cooked rice, sausage, celery leaves, sausage drippings, parsley, onion, poultry seasoning, salt, and pepper in a bowl and stir well.

Stuff the mixture into the pockets you created in the pork chops.

Bake, covered, for about 1½–2 hours.

About 15 minutes before the chops are done, remove the cover to allow them to brown on top.

Mushroom Swiss Chopped Steak

Preparation Time: 15 minutes

Cooking Time: 3 hours 30 minutes

Serving: 4

Ingredients:

1 pound ground sirloin, shaped into 4 patties

1 tablespoon butter

Salt to taste

Pepper to taste

4 slices Swiss cheese

¼ small onion, sliced

1 pound mushrooms, sliced

1 (14½-ounce) can beef gravy (or equivalent package)

Directions:

Season the sirloin patties with salt and pepper, then cook to the desired temperature. You can grill, broil, fry, or even bake the ground meat; the choice is yours.

Transfer the cooked patties to a plate and top each one with a slice of Swiss cheese.

Sauté the mushrooms and onion in a skillet (if you cooked the patties on the stovetop, use the same skillet). When the onions are translucent, add the beef gravy.

Top each patty with the onion, mushroom, and beef gravy mixture.

Chapter 7: Fish and Seafood

Chi-Chi's Seafood Chimichanga

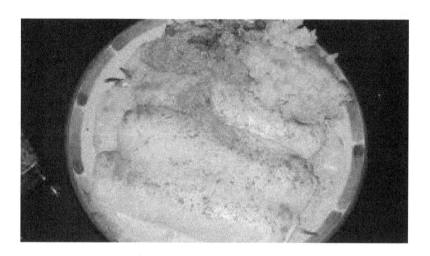

Preparation Time: 15 minutes

Cooking Time: 30 minutes

Serving: 4

Ingredients:

4 tablespoons butter

4 tablespoons flour

½ teaspoon butter

2 dashes black pepper, ground

2 cups milk

8 ounces jack cheese, shredded

1 16-ounce package crab meat, flaked

1 cup cottage cheese

¼ cup Parmesan cheese

1 egg

1 tablespoon dried parsley flakes

¼ teaspoon onion powder

1 tablespoon lemon juice

Shredded lettuce for serving

¼ cup sliced green onions for garnish

Directions:

Preheat oven to 375°F.

To make the sauce, heat butter in a pan on medium heat. Add flour, salt, and pepper. Mix, then pour in milk. Stirring often, cook until sauce is thick then simmer for an additional 1 minute.

Turn off heat and stir in jack cheese until completely blended into sauce.

In a bowl, combine crab meat, cottage and Parmesan cheese, egg, parsley, and onion powder. Heat tortillas in microwave for 10 seconds or until warm. Wet bottom side of tortilla and add crab meat mixture on top. Fold tortilla to wrap filling.

Coat baking sheet with cooking spray. Bake chimichangas for about 25 minutes.

Reheat sauce until warm. Mix in lemon juice and stir until blended.

Transfer chimichangas to plates over a bed of shredded lettuce, if desired. Top with sauce and garnish with green onions before serving.

Red Lobster's Copycat Lobster Pizza

Delicious lobster meat, melted cheeses, and parsley in a to-die-for seasoning all on a crispy tortilla—how could this not be your new favorite pizza?

Preparation Time: 15 minutes
Cooking Time: 30 minutes

Serving: 4

Ingredients:

1 10-inch flour tortillas

1 ounce roasted garlic butter

2 tablespoons Parmesan cheese, shredded

1/2 cup fresh Roma tomatoes, finely chopped

2 tablespoons fresh basil, cut into thin strips

2 ounces lobster meat, chopped

½ cup Italian cheese blend, grated

Vegetable oil for coating

Dash salt and pepper

Fresh lemon juice for serving

Directions:

Preheat oven to 450°F.

Coat one side of tortilla with garlic butter. Top with Parmesan cheese, tomatoes, basil, lobster meat, and Italian cheese blend in that order. Set aside.

Prepare a pizza pan. Apply a light coat of vegetable oil and cover with a dash of salt and pepper. Transfer pizza onto pan. Bake for about 5 minutes.

Cut into slices and drizzle with lemon juice.

Serve.

Tilapia Florentine

Preparation Time: 15 minutes
Cooking Time: 30 minutes

Serving: 4

Ingredients:

One package (6 ounces) fresh baby spinach

Six teaspoons canola oil, divided

Four tilapia fillets (4 ounces each)

One egg, lightly beaten

2 tablespoons lime juice

Two teaspoons garlic-herb seasoning blend

1/4 cup grated Parmesan cheese

1/2 cup part-skim ricotta cheese

Directions:

Cook the spinach in 4 teaspoons of oil until wilted in a large nonstick skillet; drain. In the meantime, put tilapia in a fattened 13-in. x in 9. Baking platter. Drizzle with remaining lime juice and oil. Sprinkle with a blend to season.

Combine the egg, ricotta cheese and spinach in a small bowl; spoon filets over. Sprinkle with a cheese made with Parmesan.

Bake for 15-20 minutes at 375 °, or quickly with a fork until the fish flakes.

Chapter 8: Vegetarian

Boston Market's Squash Casserole

Preparation	**Time:**	**15**	**minutes**
Cooking Time: 30 minutes			
Serving: 4			

Ingredients:

Vegetable oil for coating

1 8½-ounce box corn muffin mix

4½ cup zucchini, finely chopped

4½ cup summer squash, finely chopped

⅓ cup butter

1½ cups yellow onion, minced

1 teaspoon salt

½ teaspoon black pepper, ground

½ teaspoon thyme

1 tablespoon fresh parsley, sliced

2 chicken bouillon cubes

1 teaspoon garlic, finely chopped

8 ounces cheddar cheese, chopped

Directions:

Preheat oven to 350°F and lightly coat baking tray with vegetable oil.

Follow package instructions to cook corn muffins. Set aside.

In a deep pan, add zucchini and summer squash. Pour water into pan, enough to cover vegetables. Simmer over medium-low heat or until vegetables are soft. Add cooked squash mixture into a container along with 1 cup of the cooking water. Reserve for later. Discard remaining liquids.

Return pan to heat. Melt butter, then stir-fry onions until fragrant. Add salt, pepper, thyme, and parsley. Stir in chicken bouillon cubes, garlic, cooked squash and zucchini mixture, and cheese. Sprinkle with crumbled corn muffins. Stir everything together until well-blended, then pour onto baking tray and cover with tinfoil.

Cook in oven for about 40 minutes. Remove cover and bake for an additional 20 minutes.

Serve hot.

DIY Sweet Potato Casserole from Ruth's Chris

Preparation Time: 15 minutes

Cooking Time: 30 minutes

Serving: 4

Ingredients:

2 large sweet potatoes covered in aluminum foil

⅓ cup plus 3 tablespoons butter, divided

2 tablespoons half and half

Salt, to taste

½ cup brown sugar

¼ cup all-purpose flour

1 cup pecans, diced

Directions:

Preheat oven to 350°F.

Place sweet potatoes onto a baking tray and bake for about 60 minutes. Remove from oven.

In a bowl, add baked sweet potatoes, 3 tablespoons butter, half and half, and salt. Mash until well blended. In a separate bowl, combine pecans, brown sugar, flour, and remaining butter.

Transfer mashed sweet potatoes into a casserole dish, then top with pecan mixture. Place in oven and bake for about 20 minutes until edges bubble and pecan topping is slightly brown. Serve.

Olive Garden's Salad and Creamy Dressing

Preparation Time: 15 minutes

Cooking Time: 30 minutes

Serving: 4

Ingredients:

Dressing:

1 cup mayonnaise

⅔ cup white vinegar

5 teaspoons granulated sugar

2 tablespoons lemon juice

1 tablespoon water

⅔ cup Parmesan-Romano cheese blend

2 teaspoons olive oil

1 teaspoon Italian seasoning

1 teaspoon parsley flakes

½ teaspoon garlic salt

Salad:

1 bag salad blend of choice

Red onion, sliced

16-20 pitted black olives, sliced

Pepperoncini

Roma tomato, sliced

Croutons

Parmesan cheese, shredded

Directions:

To make the dressing, add mayonnaise, white vinegar, sugar, lemon juice, water, cheese blend, olive oil, Italian seasoning, parsley, and garlic salt to a blender. Pulse until well combined. Store in refrigerator. Ready to serve after at least 2 hours.

Assemble salad by layering salad blend, red onion, black olives, pepperoncini, tomato, croutons, and Parmesan cheese in a bowl.

Serve.

Chapter 9: Bread and Soups

Chicken Enchilada Soup

Preparation Time: 10 minutes

Cooking Time: 15 minutes

Servings: 10

Ingredients:

2 rotisserie chickens or 3 pounds cooked diced chicken

½ pound processed American cheese; cut in small cubes

3 cups yellow onions, diced

¼ cup chicken base

2 cups masa harina

½ teaspoon cayenne pepper

2 teaspoon granulated garlic

1 - 2 teaspoons salt or to taste

2 cups tomatoes, crushed

½ cup vegetable oil

2 teaspoon chili powder

4 quarts water

2 teaspoon ground cumin

Directions:

Over moderate heat in a large pot; combine oil together with onions, chicken base, granulated garlic, chili powder, cumin, cayenne & salt. Cook for 3 to 5 minutes, until onions are soft & turn translucent, stirring occasionally.

Combine 1 quart of water with masa harina in a large measuring cup or pitcher.

Continue to stir until no lumps remain. Add to the onions; bring the mixture to a boil, over moderate heat.

Once done, cook for a couple of minutes, stirring constantly. Stir in the tomatoes & leftover 3 quarts of water. Bring the soup to a boil again, stirring every now and then. Add in the cheese.

Cook until the cheese is completely melted, stirring occasionally. Add the chicken & cook until heated through. Serve immediately & enjoy.

Olive Garden Pasta Roma Soup

Preparation Time: 15 minutes

Cooking Time: 60 minutes

Serving: 4

Ingredients:

2 (16-ounce) cans drained garbanzo beans

1 cup julienned carrots

1/3 cup olive oil ¾ cup diced onions

¼ teaspoon minced garlic

1 cup diced celery

6 slices cooked bacon

1 quart chicken broth

1½ cups canned drained chopped tomatoes

½ teaspoon black pepper

2 tablespoons chopped fresh parsley

1/8 teaspoon ground rosemary ½ cup cooked macaroni

Directions:

1. Add the beans to a food processor and process until the beans mash properly.

2. Steam up the oil in a large pot. Add the carrots, onions, celery, and garlic and sauté over medium heat for 5 minutes.

3. Add remaining ingredients to the pot except for pasta. Bring this all to a boil. Reduce heat to a simmer and cook, stirring regularly, for 20 minutes.

4. Add the pasta to the finished soup and straight right away.

Chicken Tortilla Soup

Preparation Time: 10 minutes

Cooking Time: 30 minutes

Servings: 2

Ingredients:

1 chicken breast; chopped into small pieces

½ cup sweet corn

1 cup onion, chopped

3 tablespoon fresh cilantro, chopped

1 cup chicken broth

Avocado to taste

1 can diced chilies & tomatoes (8ounces)

Colby Jack cheese to taste

1 squirt of lime juice in individual bowl

Tortilla chips to taste

1 cup water

Directions:

Over moderate heat in a large, deep pot; combine the chicken broth together with water, onion, chili and tomatoes, corn and cilantro; bring the mixture to a boil, stirring occasionally.

Add in the chicken pieces; give it a good stir and decrease the heat to a simmer.

Cook for a couple of minutes, until the chicken is cooked through.

Add Tortilla chips followed by avocado & cheese to taste in serving bowls.

Add soup & a squirt of lime to the bowls. Serve hot & enjoy.

Tuscan Tomato Bisque

Preparation Time: 10 minutes
Cooking Time: 20 minutes
Servings: 4

Ingredients:

4 garlic cloves, crushed

1 can chicken broth (14 ½ ounce), undiluted

2 cans no-salt-added diced tomatoes (14 ½ ounces each), undrained

1 teaspoon olive oil

4 -5 teaspoons parmesan cheese, grated

1 tablespoon balsamic vinegar

2 ½ cups 1" French bread cubes (2 ½ slices)

1 ½ teaspoons parsley flakes, dried

Olive oil flavored cooking spray

1 teaspoon oregano, dried

½ teaspoon pepper

Directions:

Arrange bread cubes on a baking sheet in a single layer & coat the bread lightly with the cooking spray.

Bake until dry & toasted, for 8 to 10 minutes, at 400 F.

Now, over medium-low heat in large saucepan; heat the olive oil.

Once hot; add and sauté the garlic for 2 minutes.

Add the leftover ingredients (except grated parmesan cheese) & bring the mixture to a boil.

Decrease the heat & let simmer for 10 minutes, stirring every now and then.

Evenly divide the croutons among 4 to 5 bowls; ladle the soup over & sprinkle with the grated parmesan cheese. Serve immediately & enjoy.

Chapter 10: Desserts

Panera Bread® Butterscotch Bread Pudding with Bourbon & Pecans

Preparation Time: 15 minutes

Cooking Time: 55 minutes

Servings: 10 persons

Ingredients for Pudding:

5 eggs, large

1 pound rustic white bread, day-old

1 ½ cups plus 2 tablespoons sugar

2 cups pecan pieces

½ vanilla bean, split lengthwise

1 ½ tablespoons poppy seeds

3 tablespoons bourbon

½ cup melted butter, unsalted (1 stick)

4 cups heavy cream

Pinch of kosher salt

For Butterscotch Sauce:

3 tablespoons butter, unsalted

1 tablespoon bourbon

½ cup light corn syrup

1 cup light brown sugar (packed)

½ cup heavy cream

1 ½ teaspoons kosher salt

Directions:

For Butterscotch Sauce:

Over medium-high heat settings in a medium sized saucepan; bring butter, brown sugar, corn syrup & salt to a boil, whisk well until the sugar is completely dissolved. Boil for a couple of minutes, until the mixture is syrupy & measures approximately 1 and 1/3 cups. Remove the saucepan from heat & add in the bourbon and cream; stir until smooth, for couple of minutes. Let completely cool at room temperature. Cover & let chill but when ready to use, re-warm it again.

For Pudding:

Remove the crusts from the white bread & then cut it into ½" cubes. In a large sized bowl; toss bread together with 2 tablespoons of sugar & melted butter; set aside. Beat eggs & the leftover 1 and 1/2 cups of sugar in a separate large sized bowl using an electric mixer for couple of minutes, until turn pale yellow & fluffy. Add in the poppy seeds, cream & salt; beat several times to blend.

Place the bourbon in a small sized bowl; scrape in the seeds from vanilla bean. Whisk well & then add it to the egg mixture; whisk well to blend. Pour the egg mixture on top of the bread mixture in the bowl. Add in the pecans & toss several times until evenly coated. Transfer everything to a 13x9x2" ceramic or glass baking dish & spread it out in an even layer. Using a plastic wrap cover & let chill for overnight.

Remove the plastic wrap, preheat your oven to 325 F & bake for 1 & ¼ hours to 1 & 1/2 hours, until top is browned in spots. Serve the bread pudding with the butterscotch sauce.

Chocolate Chip Pizookie

Preparation Time: 20 minutes

Cooking Time: 35 minutes

Servings: 4

Ingredients:

1 cup unsalted butter, softened

½ cup brown sugar, packed

1 tablespoon vanilla

2 large eggs

½ cup chocolate covered caramel candies

1 cup sugar

2 ¾ cup flour

1 teaspoon baking soda

½ cup milk chocolate chips

1 cup semisweet chocolate chips

½ teaspoon salt

Directions:

Preheat your oven to 350 F in advance & lightly coat a 10" cast iron skillet with the baking spray.

Cream the butter with sugar & brown sugar in your stand mixer for a minute or two, until pale & fluffy, on high.

Add in the eggs and vanilla; continue to combine on medium speed until completely incorporated.

Add in the baking soda, flour & salt until just combined then fold in the chocolates.

Put half of the cookie dough into the cast iron skillet & sprinkle in the chocolate covered caramels; cover with the leftover cookie dough & bake in the preheated oven for 20 minutes, covered with foil. Uncover & bake for 10 more minutes.

Starbucks' Chocolate Cinnamon Bread

Preparation Time: 15 minutes

Cooking Time: 1 hour

Servings: 16

Ingredients:

Bread:

1½ cups unsalted butter

3 cups granulated sugar

5 large eggs

2 cups flour

1¼ cups processed cocoa

1 tablespoon ground cinnamon

1 teaspoon salt

½ teaspoon baking powder

½ teaspoon baking soda

¼ cup water

1 cup buttermilk

1 teaspoon vanilla extract

Topping:

¼ cup granulated sugar

½ teaspoon cinnamon

½ teaspoon processed cocoa

⅛ teaspoon ginger, ground

⅛ teaspoon cloves, ground

Directions:

Before cooking:

Preheat the oven to 350°F;

Grease two 9×5×3 loaf pans; and

Line the bottoms of the pans with wax paper.

Cream the sugar by beating it with the butter.

Beat the eggs into the mixture one at a time.

When the mixture starts becoming doughy, divide it in two and transfer it to the pans.

Mix together all the topping ingredients and sprinkle evenly on top of the mixture in both pans.

Bake for 50 to 60 minutes, or until the bread has set.

Royal Dansk Butter Cookies

Preparation Time: 15 minutes

Cooking Time: 25 minutes

Servings: 10

Ingredients:

120g cake flour, sifted

½ teaspoon vanilla extract

25g powdered sugar

120g softened butter, at room temperature

A pinch of sea salt, approximately ¼ teaspoon

Directions:

Using a hand mixer; beat the butter with sugar, vanilla & salt until almost doubled in mass & lightened to a yellowish-white in color, for 8 to 10 minutes, on low to middle speed.

Scrape the mixture from the sides of your bowl using a rubber spatula. Sift the flour x 3 times & gently fold in until well incorporated.

Transfer the mixture into a sheet of plastic wrap, roll into log & cut a hole on it; placing it into the piping bag attached with a nozzle flower tips 4.6cm/1.81" x 1.18".

Pipe each cookie into 5cm wide swirls on a parchment paper lined baking tray.

Cover & place them in a freezer until firm up, for 30 minutes.

Preheat your oven to 300 F in advance. Once done; bake until the edges start to turn golden, for 20 minutes.

Let completely cool on the cooling rack before serving.

Store them in an airtight container.

TGI Friday's Oreo Madness

Preparation Time: 15 minutes

Cooking Time: 30 minutes

Serving: 4

Ingredients:

1 (14-ounce) package Oreo cookies

½ cup (1 stick) butter, melted

5 cups vanilla ice cream

For drizzling: hot fudge and caramel toppings

Directions:

Line muffin pans with cupcake liners.

If needed, let ice cream stand at room temperature to soften a little, for easier spreading.

Place Oreos in a blender or food processor and pulse to break into crumbs.

Transfer to a bowl and stir in melted butter. Mix well.

Press about 2 tablespoons each of crumb mixture into muffin tins.

Top each with about ¼ cup ice cream, smoothening down with a spatula.

Cover with another 2 tablespoons of crumbs.

Cover and freeze until set (about 2 hours).

Remove from muffin tins.

Drizzle with toppings and serve.

Conclusion

Through making these dishes yourself rather than eating out, you'll just see how much you actually saved for each dish and you'll understand what I am talking about. Remember, don't limit yourself and experiment, be creative and have fun!

You might find yourself in the situation of not being able or willing to go to your favorite restaurant to enjoy some of the delicious meals they serve there.

So reproducing them at home will be the best way to always enjoy them!

Train consistently and keep following me!

thank you and enjoy!

CPSIA information can be obtained
at www.ICGtesting.com
Printed in the USA
BVHW062330220321
603180BV00003B/368